# Bards Against Hunger

## New Jersey

### New Jersey Bards

Bards Against Hunger

Copyright © 2019 by New Jersey Bards

Published by Local Gems Press

www.localgemspoetrypress.com

All rights reserved. No part of this book may be reproduced or transmitted in any form or by any means without written permission of the authors.

*Dedicated to everyone who ever wondered where their next meal was coming from, and those who aim to lend a helping hand.*

# Foreword

Bards Against Hunger was founded in 2013 by the Bards Initiative, a poetry group on Long Island, NY that hosts many readings and publishes local anthologies. The leaders of this group came up with the idea to host a poetry reading that would gather food for the hungry around Thanksgiving time as a way for poets to give back to their local community. The poets of Long Island loved the idea and flocked to help organize, read at the event, and gather food.

The event was such a success that the group decided to make it an annual event--and keep the tradition strong and growing each year.

In 2015, NoVA Bards, a sister poetry group to the Bards Initiative of NY started a corresponding Bards Against Hunger down in Fairfax, Northern Virginia. The poets of the NoVA Bards group did the same thing--came together for a reading and raised food for a local pantry. The poets of Long Island were excited to know that the tradition was being held in another state as well, and it gave us the idea that this simple yet effective idea could be very easy replicated in other parts of the country.

In the following year, thanks to inter-state poetry connectivity through Local Gems Poetry Pres, Bards Against Hunger was set to happen in 5 states and groups in other areas expressed interest in adopting the tradition as well.

To date, Bards Against Hunger has now run events in over a dozen US states and even had corresponding events in other countries. Every year we raise thousands of pounds of food to be donated to local food banks.

This year, for the first time, we host a reading in New Jersey, and are happy to welcome them into the fold.

# Table of Contents

Robb Bosman ............................................................................ 1
Jamie Capach ............................................................................ 3
Jeannie Chapkowski ................................................................. 5
Bonny Collins ........................................................................... 7
Christine Cote .......................................................................... 9
Gary S. Crawford ................................................................... 11
Penelope Daniels ................................................................... 17
Liza DeStefano ...................................................................... 19
Lynette Esposito .................................................................... 20
Melody Francis ...................................................................... 22
Ashima Hosalkar ................................................................... 23
Carole Leskin ........................................................................ 25
Bernadette LoPinto-Neil ....................................................... 28
C.E. McAuley ........................................................................ 31
Kathy Moore .......................................................................... 34
Courtney Noel ....................................................................... 36
Tom Pawlowski ..................................................................... 38
Yvonne Plyshette .................................................................. 40
David Porter .......................................................................... 43
Daniel H. Ramos ................................................................... 45
Karen Lee Ramos .................................................................. 47

Christine L. Rusin .................................................................. 49

Sofia Senesie ........................................................................ 51

Danny Scully ........................................................................ 53

George Scully ....................................................................... 55

Linda Scully ......................................................................... 58

Nashunda Squier .................................................................. 60

Sarah Squire ......................................................................... 62

Maria Taney ......................................................................... 64

Lorraine DiPasquale Walkiewicz ........................................... 66

MM Wittle ........................................................................... 68

Paul-Victor Winters .............................................................. 70

Scott Woodland .................................................................... 72

# Robb Bosman

## Featherlight

No depth today
No books
Screaming colors yell for
Hawaiian shirts and
Coconut rum
Indulgence and paper umbrellas
Distanciated grimaces and
Lighthearted laughter
The evening oncoming with
Glee and no deep thoughts
Just love and food and
Joy and merrymaking
The supermarket a toy store for
Adulthood pleasures
And later, the books?
They got laid on another table
Unmoved

Robb Bosman is a Dutch poet, artist, living in NJ who has been writing poetry for over 30 years. Some of it is published in the Netherlands in books of poetry and his own (former) magazine "PerVerse". Everyday life and inner experiences are key to his work. In the US it is hard to focus on art when trying to make ends meet, but still; "What goes in, must come out".

# Jamie Capach

## foolhardy expedition

the mountain of dishes in my kitchen sink
has me dumbstruck with awe and
worried I will never surmount the peak
and make it back alive

the blizzard of paperwork strewn about my floor
under bureaucratic red tape like tattered prayer flags
leaves me stupefied and doubtful conditions are
good enough to leave base camp

i haven't made my bed
but i lay in it just the same
knowing it isn't rated for this deep freeze
and that it offers only false comfort
at the foot of this craggy behemoth

i fail to cry out for help
my self-compassion left me for dead
to save itself as i lay frostbitten and stiff
like so many others who perished these slopes
even before i start the ascension

it's a foolhardy expedition
to take up mountain climbing
when i can barely walk
responsibility and maturity demand it
yet my own feelings are too insurmountable
the air of depression too thin to breathe
the gravity of anxiety too heavy upon my chest

woman against the elements
rugged individualism
mountain unclimbed
chores left for
another day

---

Jamie Capach is a New Hampshire native. She lives in Chatham, New Jersey with her partner, whose two black cats begrudgingly tolerate her presence. Her art and poetry reflect her mental health recovery, her queer relationships, and her experiences as a trans woman. Her work has appeared in *Post-Traumatically Stressed Feminist*.

# Jeannie Chapkowski

## Tired Brown Couch

I am a tired brown couch
 Comforting an old man, his wife, a frightened mouse.
I am where sleeping dogs lie
Licked clean my face, fabric stitches of my eye.
I cradled soft babies as they learned to climb
Listened to sweet lullabies chanted in rhyme.
I posed for Christmas pictures
Nightly readings of bible scriptures.
Snuggled up young girls and boys
With me discovered heartaches and joys.
My tear stained arm painfully tore
Where grief spilled a mother, her son lost in war.
"Neighbor, you can sleep on the couch ,"
Always drinking himself out of his house.
 Cigarette holes burnt mystery in my back
Only I know the secret of Pappa's stolen pack.
 Now Papa said " I can't part with this couch, why, it's the best part of our house.
He's dependable you know .
"Mama argued, "it's old and raggedy, look you can see its bones In the middle it's saggy."
"Ahhh my love, just come sit next to me

But hey, while you're up please turn on the T.V. "
I am a lucky brown couch.

---

Jeannie resides in Flemington NJ. She loves to write lyrics and poetry portraying the depth of life and the human spirit.

# Bonny Collins

**When I Write**

I go deep.
I am not here, but there.
In my mind, I see and hear and feel what I am
writing about.
My life.
My thoughts and feelings.

How do those who write fiction do it?
Are they also immersed in a different time and place?
Do they experience all the emotions I feel when I read
their writing?

I write my life.
The memories I shape to help me see a story,
A beginning, a middle, and end.
A way to see a unified whole, even though it is a partial
view

Too often I get stuck
deep in the experience—
Feeling the hurt, the pain, the regret.
Why didn't I handle my life differently?

How did I miss that significant point?
I am under water, where there is danger, but also beauty.
Feeling the joy, the choices, the luck.
Why didn't I realize how wonderful a moment was?

When today calls to me,
It is as if my oxygen line has been given a tug;
I realize that there is sunshine on the surface.
I come back from a dive far below the surface

It takes a minute to breathe again
To be here and now
I look around, regrounding myself in what is
And leave behind what was,
Deep in my thoughts.

---

Bonny Ketterer Collins started teaching in 1971, mostly writing, ESL, and gifted classes, from kindergarten to community colleges, in PA, RI, OH, CA, FL, KS, and NJ, and has visited all 50 states. In Cape May County since retiring, she has found a wonderful outlet in the local writing groups who feed one another's minds.

# Christine Cote

## A Sighting

I thought at first
it was a bird.
Tiny feet stuck
to thin ice atop
the large pond.
Was the bird
trapped all night?
Frozen in place?

Or, was it just a
twig? I did not
climb down the
bank to find out.
We protect our-
selves from things,
real and imagined.

Avoid taking
that closer look.

*("A Sighting" was one of 183 poems long-listed from 1,641 total submissions by Fish Publishing in its 2019 contest judged by Billy Collins.)*

---

A Cape May County resident for over thirty years, Christine is a former attorney and journalist who has published a collection of poems entitled *A Visionary's Conceit* and is currently working on a second collection. She serves on the county's Culture and Heritage Commission and its Advisory Commission for Woman. As a board member of the Friends of Fishing Creek School in Lower Township, she helped develop a poetry contest for fifth and sixth graders, which prompted over 90 student poems to be submitted and which she hopes to expand next April.

# Gary S. Crawford

## 1949 Studebaker Pickup Truck

I was just seventeen, and had me a car,
She was a little old, wouldn't take me that far.
So I was looking for something else that I could buy.

Dad told me of a truck that he had spied,
With a For Sale sign hanging on its side,
That he thought looked good and that I should stop by.

I went to see the truck and the man,
Who was ready to sell it, as soon as he can,
I was thinking that I was finally getting some luck.

I went to see it, to check it all out,
I was glad Dad had seen it, and told me about,
A 1949 Studebaker pickup truck.

It fired right up and sounded real good,
I went to the front and opened the hood,
And looked at the engine and all the parts inside.

Just a little rust and the tires were fair,
I looked at the man and pulled back my hair,
And asked him if I could take it for a ride.

He opened the door and nodded his head,
As I jumped in his truck that was painted red,
He told me not to take it very far.

He looked around, playing it cool,
As he took out some kind of tool,
And he took the license plates right off of his car.

He hung the plates on the truck real fast,
Looking out for any cops going past,
And asked me if I knew how to drive a stick.

I told him I did, my Dad taught me how,
He liked what he heard as he wiped off his brow,
He told me to drive it, but be sure to be back real quick.

I stepped on the clutch and pulled it in gear,
Looked around me and checked in the mirror,
Then pulled out slowly onto the road.

It went right along, it had some nice power,
And I drove that truck, the man of the hour!
I was so excited, I was ready to explode.

I didn't go far and then came right back,
There was nothing about this truck that it lacked,
I had the cash ready to give to the man.

He had the title and was ready to sign,
And smiled when I said that it ran just fine,
We did the transaction and he shook my hand.

I had to get plates so I hit DMV,
I'm sure glad my friends gave a ride to me,
It cost me, but the guys are a real good bunch.

I had no problem laying out some bucks,
This was important, all for my truck,
So I sprung for some sodas and a real nice lunch.

Then we went back to pick up my ride.
We put on the plates and I jumped inside,
Anxious to take it for my first real live trip.

I started it up and commenced to drive,
Man, did I ever feel alive!
Moving along at a pretty good clip.

I drove it home, and Dad was to say,
That I made me a nice little deal that day,
As I parked the truck out back by a tree.

With buckets and sponges, a hose and some suds,
All that we needed, plus a six-pack of Buds,
We gave it a bath, all my friends and me.

She looked pretty good, all shiny and clean,
She needed some more, to make her look mean,
So we pinstriped her hood in white and black paint.

That made a difference, we all could agree,
Wait till the rest of our friends come to see,
Ordinary truck? That much she ain't.

With west coast mirrors and marker lights,
That old truck sure was a sight,
Especially when we painted flames on the hood.

Young guys we were, all ready to bop,
But not wanting to get stopped by a cop,
So around the law, we all were good.

What kind of truck is that, they would ask,
As I went to my ride to do another task,
Ready to go out and make me another buck.

My grin was big, as was my pride,
As I nodded over toward my ride,
That's my 1949 Studebaker pickup truck.

We named her "Country Comfort" after a song,
And we'd sing it while we drove along,
Everyone watching wherever we would go.

Whether out cruising or hauling some trash,
That truck was a great way to make extra cash,
She paid back what I spent in about four months or so.

Hot or cold, rain or snow,
There wasn't a place we couldn't go,
We never even came close to getting stuck.

Amps and drums for our rock band,
Or a stack of bricks or a load of sand,
In that 1949 Studebaker pickup truck.

She was a great truck, I want you to know,
When I had her, four pickups ago,
With her, I had nothing but good luck.

I sure miss her, in every way,
And I wish I still had her to this very day,
My 1949 Studebaker pickup truck.

Gary S. Crawford is an award-winning author and historian. He has published six books and many short stories and articles. He's a Jersey Shore native and lives with his wife, daughter, and four grandchildren, and is trying to be retired. He writes a blog, "Creative Bellyaching" http://garyscrawford.blogspot.com
    and his website is
www.crawsat.wixsite.com/garyscrawford.

# Penelope Daniels

*With Fire*

Face of Demeter.
Baking bread -
sick with fire.
Attempting patience.

-----------

*Antinous*

Gardens of statues -
broken monuments to Loss;
headless and armless.

-----------

*Limp of the Gods*

Peach smashed, inside out.
Arsenic-filled heart, open -
not unlike my own.

Penelope Daniels is a lifelong resident of Southern New Jersey and an avid nerd, writer, artist, gamer, costume enthusiast and rabbit lover. She also spends her free time collecting tarot cards, vintage board & role-playing games and lunchboxes. When she's not pursuing her hobbies or adding to her collections, she can be found at Farpoint Toys & Collectibles - the toy & comic store she owns with her husband in the Jersey Pine Barrens.

# Liza DeStefano

## Paved in Gold

Paths of life brilliantly sparkling with light.
Reflections holding you back not right…
Gather all thoughts put on a shelf.
Use the heart to follow oneself…
Walking alone we all must do.
Bad thinking not wanting to accrue…
Longing for the right moment to burst.
Let it happen quench the thirst…
Always imagine how the path will feel.
Can it really be real…?
No answer nowhere to be found.
The mind needs to be spellbound

---

Liza DeStefano is a poet and author of two books Wings of my heart and Lighting the Way. Her poetry is raw and relatable dealing with loss and life events. Liza resides in South Jersey with her family.

# Lynette Esposito

## Old Family Recipes

The book leans
against the shelf.
Stained,
Struggling for balance
with a slight spill of egg white
and pepper
intermixed with
pictures of
successful fruit salad
and Salisbury steak.

It was my grandmother's Bible
in the kitchen; then
my mother's, now mine.

I don't use it.

I remember

how to sift the flower,
separate the yolks,
add a pinch of this

to that,
stir the chicken dumplings,
holler for everyone to come.

I remember
how to fill the house with
home.

---

Lynette G. Esposito, MA Rutgers, has been published in Fox Chase Review North of Oxford, That Literary Review, Edify,, Remembered Arts, South Jersey Bards, Burlington County Bards, and others. She is an advocate of feeding the hungry. She was married to Attilio Esposito and lives in Southern New Jersey.

# Melody Francis

**Reassurance**

I felt like I was outside
in the dead of winter
with no coat or boots on

alone

until I read your reassuring letter

then, it was like
we were sitting in
a cozy living room
by a fire, enjoying
each other's company
cheerfully sipping
cups of hot chocolate

---

Melody lives in northern NJ with her family and pets. She has been writing poetry for years and hopes to put together her own anthology someday. If a poem makes someone smile or feel something relatable, she is happy.

# Ashima Hosalkar

**Tree**

A far distant tree,
stands tall and all green;
be it any season,
or any weather,
but that one – always
a sight of glee.

The little squirrel
dashes uphill-downhill
on its limbs strong and free;
playing around with
an acorn or two;
hiding gleefully behind
those leaves of three.

Its cozy twigs and sprigs,
a little abode to
the birds
flighting across in spree.

It gives away all its
everything; its very being
to all those around;
including me.

why we, humans,
still ask for more and strip
ourselves of these blessings;
with
a cowardly and dastardly
blow of a machete;
a grim reaper slitting
a throat of its own!

---

Ashima Hosalkar is a poet and a writer, who grew up in India and lives in Basking Ridge; she likes to call herself as an illegitimate poet. She enjoys writing and likes to capture and convey raw human emotions, the beauty of nature, and voice for social cause. Her work has appeared in NJ Bards Northwestern Poetry Review and We Are Beat National Beat Poetry Foundation Inc Anthologies.

# Carole Leskin

## Carole's' Debate

"You are old", says the voice in my head.
"You have many years left", says my beating heart.

"You are slowing down - it's to be expected", says the voice in my head.
"You have so much left to see and do", says my beating heart.

"You must prepare for the limitations to come", says the voice in my head.
"You should be open to new opportunities and adventures", says my beating heart.

"You must act your age - let your hair grow gray", says the voice in my head.
"You should do as you please", says my beating heart.

"You must be strong and self-reliant", says the voice in my head.
"You should not hesitate to ask for help when you need it", says my beating heart.

"You must be ever vigilant for it is a dangerous world", says the voice in my head.
"You should welcome and be grateful for the kindness of strangers", says my beating heart.

"You must learn to live with loss", says the voice in my head.
"You should view each day as a new beginning", says my beating heart.

"You must come to terms with the Inevitability Of Death", says the voice in my head.
"You should find Purpose and Joy in Life", says my beating heart.

The debate is intense. When it concludes, who is the winner? My head or my heart?

Can both be right?

Carole Leskin is a retired Director of Global Human Resources. Embarking on a second career as a writer and photographer concentrating on her personal accounts of aging, her essays and poetry, frequently accompanied by her photos, are published regularly in Jewish Sacred Aging and Starts At 60 and recently in Time Goes By. Her poem, Father Time, was selected for inclusion in the 2019 anthology of poetry, New Jersey Bards. She is the founder of the blog YBAlone which focuses on the challenges of growing older, especially for those who live alone with no family or support system, an issue which impacts her personally.

# Bernadette LoPinto-Neil

## Looking at Photos on the Eve of Our 36th Anniversary

*Atlantic City 1967*
In this snapshot,
I'm four and squinting
into a low-slung sun.
I am lit golden and wrapped
in a souvenir sweatshirt
covered in tiny pictures
of nautical flags.
Each, I imagine,
signaled a small disaster
I'd soon endure.

*Atlantic City 1981*
I'm in love and looking down.
You are whispering
something into my ear
that I've long forgotten.
This shot was snipped
from a strip of four,
taken in a boardwalk
booth, back when
the rising casinos
promised
to lift all boats.

*Atlantic City 2019*
We are driving
through derelict
streets in search
of something familiar.
Letters have been
pried from the side
of a disused garage
to protect the names
of the insolent.

On the boardwalk,
we walk arm in arm.
Three dozen years
have rolled by as swiftly
as these storm clouds
now pressing in on us.

Your love is buoyant.
It keeps me afloat
in an ocean of itself.
Am I sinking or saved
depends
on how
I want to tell it.

(For Robert)

Bernadette is a teacher trainer from Wall Township, NJ. As an undergraduate at TCNJ, she was the founding editor of The Siren: Voices from the Lifespan, a literary magazine that published poetry and short stories from both students and faculty writers. She lives near the Jersey Shore with her husband, Robert.

# C.E. McAuley

## Papa

I often wonder
What thoughts were
Going through your
Head

While you sat
In your easy chair
Watching baseball
And not following
The games.

Were they back
In Brooklyn?

Your mind in New Guinea
Taking shrapnel
And picking up pieces
Of your dead friends
Just enough
Left to send
Home in
Cigar boxes?

Was it the
Army doctors
Giving you electroshock
When you became catatonic
After you washed
Up on the beach
When you, treated for
Malaria, swam past the
Japanese and waved,
Them taking you
For you for one of
Their own?

Was it Lake Champlain
And your grandmother
The piano teacher?

Your only moments
Of happiness?

What were you thinking at
The crack of the bat
Ball roaring
Soaring so far
Into the sky?

C.E. McAuley was born in New Brunswick, NJ and lives in Mercer County where he teaches college English and is a Literacy New Jersey ESL volunteer tutor and teacher.

# Kathy Moore

**Which is the Right Way to Write**

Tap, tap,
Sharpen pencil
Erase words
Smudge
Crumple

Tap, Tap
Clean keyboard
Copy, paste
Backspace
Delete

Which is the right way to write?

Tick, toc
Free Write
Use Prompts
Outside
Inside
Which is the right way to write?

Tic toc

Align alliteration
Rhyming verse
Conjugate
Limerick
Which is the right way to write?

Moan groan
Lunch time
Laundry piled
Bills
 Nap
Not the right way to write!

Tap, tap
Sit down
Focus
Ideas
Words
Finally, the right way to write!

---

Kathy Moore, a year-round resident of Cape May County, is a graduate of Stockton University and currently works as a library assistant for the Cape May County Library. She blogs about her daily blessings at http://kathswriting.blogspot.com/. She lives by the motto "Take time to watch a sunset."

# Courtney Noel

**to the one i lost to suicide**

i've always imagined heaven to be
a place above the clouds, right before outer space begins
with soft cumulus floors – why else would the angels walk
around barefoot all of the time?
a place where everything is white but not like a hospital;
not in a painful way that's too bright to look at
but in a way that's soft and soothing
a place with gates made of gold that rise higher than you could
ever see that greet you upon arrival
followed by a soothing voice telling you that everything is
going to be okay now
i wonder if that's where you are now
i wonder if you're a piece of blue sky during the day
or if you're one of the stars in the night sky
i wonder if you're somewhere no one can comprehend
or if you're much closer to me than i realize
wherever you are
i just hope it's nice
i hope that, if heaven is real and if you're there, that it's
everything better than anything i've imagined
but more importantly

i just hope that you're there, and that you're happy, and that it's treating you better than living on earth did

Courtney is a twenty-five year old South Jersey native, residing in Cumberland County. She is a self-published poet with her debut collection "Have Some Pride" available now on Amazon. "to the one i lost to suicide" is a poem featured in her sophomore poetry collection "Stay Alive" which is a current work in progress.

# Tom Pawlowski

## Walnut Street

Homeless man with cat
Settles in for the cold night
Keep each other warm

## Hush

As dark is to light
It's moments of silence that
Put sounds in context

## My Country

Without puffery
Spirit of America
Shines through compassion

Tom Pawlowski (tomp) is a life-long resident of South Jersey. In 2012 he made a New Year's resolution to write a haiku everyday, and he hasn't stopped yet. Daily exercise / Seventeen short syllables / Some better than most. His day job is in engineering.

# Yvonne Plyshette

**Sunrise**

On my darkest days
The sun didn't shine
I watched it rise
I searched for sun rays
But I was left in a daze
Searching for ways
Looking for sun rays
Unsure of my ways
Lost in loss for days
It felt like the sun didn't shine for days
I wanted to see it, I should see it
I certainly sensed it

A new dawn, a new day
The beautiful sun was there
But darkness blocked my way

Until the Son
Reminded me that He is The One
The only begotten Son
"I created the sun

I told it to rise
Stop believing lies
The Son has risen
The sun does rise"

I stood at sunrise
I watched the sun rise
I think, I pray, I realize
I am in awe of God's creation
With joy and elation
I marvel at His might
The Son turns darkness into light
The sun turns darkness into light

On my darkest days
He is my sun rays

At sunrise
I watch the sun rise
I remember, the Son did rise
I thank the Son
For sunrise

Yvonne Plyshette, widowed mother of two, began writing poems and short stories when she was in grade school. Her love for writing complements her career as a grant writer and consultant. After her husband Kenny's unexpected death, Plyshette began publicly sharing her poetry and writing in a blog, "I Am Living Through It: And You can too ([wordpress.com](wordpress.com))!" Through her writings and blog, Plyshette shares her grief journey by illustrating God's love and offering hope and encouragement to others.

# David Porter

## Torch Town Eulogy

It had to burn.
Even without paper,
it was incendiary.
The numbers,
once subtracted,
only coughed,
unwilling to say their unbearable sum aloud.
The days were unstruck match heads.
The nights wheezed,
starved for air.

Afterward,
we sat in bed
and picked through the cinders.
There was a laminated map of Venice,
my grandfather's wedding ring,
a crescent of green glass
we found on a beach near Mykonos Town,
a horn concerto…
We had pawned everything else.

Across the street,
in the courtyard of a smoldering building
smoke still whispering from its roof,
a little boy flung
fistfuls of feathery ashes
toward a waning streetlight.

---

David A. Porter is a graduate of Rutgers University and San Francisco State University, where he received his MFA in Creative Writing. Porter was a co-founder and the managing editor of *20 Pounds of Headlights*, a literary annual published in San Francisco in 2004. He lives in New York, where he is working on a collection of short stories, *Protracted Adolescence*, a collection of poems, *Ghost Season*, and a non-fiction book about music, *20,000 Things I Love*.

# Daniel H. Ramos

**Moving Stones**

Even stones are moving every second
made up of spinning molecules.
When you kick them
they move even more.

Sitting on a huge rock
looking at a beautiful waterfall
I put my hand in the flow
felt stones tumbling down
from the top of the cliff
into the river below.

I had a bunch of pebbles in my hand
with a shiny glow
because they were wet
they looked so beautiful
in the sun gazing down on us.

When I climbed off the huge rock
it wiggled
like the trembling of going down a ladder.
It was moving

like everything.
I like that rock
I come this way often.

---

Daniel H. Ramos is an award winning poet and visual artist. His poetry has been displayed in New Jersey's Paterson Museum and was published in The Stillwater Review as well as the Paulinskill Poetry Project anthology Voices From Here 2. Daniel is thirteen years old.

# Karen Lee Ramos

## Marsh House

Trees take turns with the wind
as the tide comes in
two arms of saltwater embrace
touching at the narrow bridge.

Water flows through salt grasses
in a web of branching veins
that rise
until road and marsh become bay.

Birds arrive
geese and laughing gulls
the arrow of a heron
glides above the reunited inlet.

At low tide the moors empty again
the rutted road returns
combed with sunlight
damp grasses become golden.

I want to memorize these patterns
of wind and water and light

but all I can do is watch them
come and go

until the call of an unseen owl
ushers in twilight.

---

Karen Lee Ramos hosts POETRY at the BARN, a reading series & writing program located in the Barn Gallery of Ringwood State Park, NJ. Her poetry appears in publications such as Paterson Literary Review, Exit 13 and The Stillwater Review. Contact Karen at klrpoetry@yahoo.com

# Christine L. Rusin

## Screaming On The Inside

I am SCREAMING
S-C-R-E-A-M-I-N-G
SCREAMING on the inside

I am burning up
Scorches
Sweaty
Dripping with rage
Shaking with age

Lost in the heat and fire
Imploding with desire
To right a wrong
To wrong a right

I am S-M-I-L-I-N-G
Smiling
Smiling some more

I am calm
Cool
Motionless

E-MOTIONLESS

Still Sweating
Still Raging
STILL SCREAMING IN SILENCE

I am screaming
Screaming on the inside

Lost in a noisy world
That is loud enough
Without me

---

Christine L. Rusin is an award-winning writer, filmmaker, and photographer. Since childhood she has explored the themes of light and dark in her art and writing. Christine has produced and directed over 500 films since 1985. Her short narrative movies have been screened internationally and have received multiple awards. When not working on artistic ventures, she is restoring an historic farm and trains hunting dogs for competition. Her media company PARASHOOT PRODUCTIONS is located in Hope, New Jersey. She can be reached at parashoot@me.com

# Sofia Senesie

## April 22

Night I've found I cannot sleep,
And my bedroom becomes a ruthless desert.
It's so frequent needn't I be bothered to weep,
And rather forced to have my eyes open and alert.
Hours pass, the clock keeps hissing,
And I can't put my finger on what it is I'm missing.

Not a camel in sight in this desert it seems,
But a burning sun of desperation.
And the subject of water is a thing of dreams,
Depriving an entire nation,
Desperately hoping to extract water from the air,
Hours and hours into the sky we stare.

The later the hour, the cooler the desert grows,
My mind slips into the chill oasis,
And the sand man blows
'For which is the basis.
'Tis at last a desert illusion to which I am plucky,
If such luck exists, we could only be so lucky.

Sofia Senesie is a young writer in love with writing and the voice it gives her as well as others. Everyone has a story to tell. She loves to tell stories to make everyone's day a bit brighter.

# Danny Scully

## A Sonnet to my Loved Ones

Trust lies that within your eyes
Comfort ever present in your actions
Being a beacon for me when tides are high.
A soul of protection causes reactions
Shouting is heard as the skies cry,
yet you still stand by my side
The storms halt and the rain dies
By and by are the words left behind, when all of your voice guides.
Guides me to safety as time flies, the worries die when you are at my side.
Mind ever wondering how you came into my life, a loving feeling that lies within
Crying is the sky a reaction so benign, your eyes warm and kind brings me to the light.
Bright is this feeling that I try to tell, maybe you would understand if I sang it well.
Words often fail and stutter out my voice isn't strong so I will have to shout
Well is a word that I don't often fathom and when I speak the Phantom of a voice comes out

But still I will try to tell you all of the reasons that you matter even if I can't exactly shout or if I lose count Without you I would be lost and That I have no doubt.

---

Danny Scully is nineteen years old and he is from a small burrow in South Jersey. He recently graduated with a degree in Fine Arts from Cumberland County College, he was apart of the last group of graduates before it became Rowan College of South Jersey. He is often found spending time with his family, reading, writing, exploring, or programming.

# George Scully

**Magic 8-Ball**

I grasped the Magic 8-Ball
And asked it if I should
Pen a verse about its charms
It told me, "Outlook good"

So, here is a rhyme, a poem
Of assured obscurity
About that sooth-saying oracle
From Milton Bradley

I started asking questions
And it put on a show
Me: Will I hit the lottery?
It: My reply is no.

So, I asked it other questions
Me, speculating if I ever could
Grow back my head of golden hair
And it said, "Outlook good"

Now according to the 8-Ball
I will not hit the lottery

But as consolation my hair grows back
Not too shabby, mon ami

So, I thought I'd bump it up a notch
I'd thrown softballs the whole time
Well now I'd throw some curve balls too
The answers should be sublime

Magic 8-Ball, why is there suffering
And justice disavowed
Why hatred, hunger, & homelessness?
It said it, "Couldn't answer now"

Now the manufactures warranty
Just won't cover such misuse
I must confine to "Yes" or "No"
No questions so obtuse

So, I put the 8-Ball on the self
The oracle does not care
I guess I'll just keep searching
For answers found elsewhere

George lives in South Jersey with his wife, his three kids—who are not kids anymore, and two dogs. He is aware that he is a lucky man and he is thankful. He knows that now everyone is so lucky, and he hopes that whatever is produced from this project—this collection of poems, will get into hands that need it. He hopes that our priorities shift as a people, as a society, and that hunger ceases to be the specter that faces so many of families today.

# Linda Scully

## Twenty Five Years

Buffeted by the winds of change
Pounded by the ocean of time
The sand of choices made and unmade shift beneath our feet
Yet, still we stand

Laughter, sadness, death, debt and stress
Joy, wonder, love and happiness
We have sacrificed a lot, but gained so much in return
Isn't life grand?

Twenty five years have come and gone
Together more than half our lives
I cannot imagine my life without you in it
Yes, we still stand

The future is unknowable
The past, well, that's in the past
So we shall continue on and adventure together
Its love's demand.

Linda Scully works in the Arts and Humanities Department of a small community college. She is constantly inspired by her family, students and faculty. When not clacking away at a keyboard, Linda can often be seen "behind-the-scenes" at student productions zipping, pinning, sewing, mothering, reprimanding...

# Nashunda Squier

## On Our Own

In an infantile state of determination
We persist
Pushing forward, struggling
In an effort to achieve

On Our Own

We fight the obstacles, the barriers
That riddle the path
Focusing on the "I"
Wanting the accolades of success
A pat on the back
Yearning so much for our worth to be seen
For recognition in what we accomplish

On Our Own

We stumble, we fall
We knock down others
And clamor over them
We crawl
In this infantile state

Rarely maturing to a point of realization
Of understanding
That we are relational and not meant to be

On Our Own

That we could attain so much more
If only we would
Reach out and offer, reach up and accept assistance
And work
Together

---

Nashunda Squier, a.k.a. Sunni, lives in Washington, NJ. She is a devoted Christian, wife and mother. She has been dedicated to the education of children for many years and is currently a Language Arts teacher. In her free time, she enjoys reading and creating art and poetry in many different forms.

# Sarah Squire

## My Fruit

Sweetness between
my finger tips
lets off an aroma
that touches
all my senses

So juicy
so delicate
a taste
which there is
no comparison

Your unique look
sets you apart from
all others
Radiant Red

You're desirable, wanted,
appreciated
by all
who experience you

You bring smiles
to many faces
you've made memories
in the minds of many

Strawberries
oh how sweet you are

---

Sarah Squire is a soul that is always looking for expansion. She loves to write poetry as a form of expression and healing on all subjects. Even though she is human she likes to believe she is a mermaid with salt water running through her veins.

Maria Taney

**The Tormentor**
    It followed me
      into the house
        and stayed close
           real close
         I swatted
       and missed
     It left me
   for a minute
    then came back again
       in my ear it hummed
         lingered at my ankles
          round and round
           stalking
       tormenting
     hungry
   enough was enough
    splat
       my blood
on the kitchen wall.

Maria Taney converted her whole yard into a pollinator garden where insects abound. She finds it hard to feel the love for mosquitos however.

# Lorraine DiPasquale Walkiewicz

**Out of Place**

I look in the mirror
And what do I see?
Someone that looks
A lot like me

But my hair is blonde
And her hair is grey.
And she's looking at me
In a sad sort of way.

The music is playing,
My mind wants to dance
But my body is saying
Oh no, not a chance.

I close my eyes
And what do I see?
The face of the young girl
I used to be.

The memory is there
I cannot erase,
The spirit in a body
That is OUT OF PLACE.

---

Lorraine is a Jersey Girl, born and raised. Her education and work experience are in Math and Finance. In her spare time she loves to read and 'visit' exotic places in her mind. Throughout her life she wrote short stories and poems as a way of coping with life's experiences. Lorraine welcomes the opportunity to participate in the NJ Bards Against Hunger cause with her poems.

# MM Wittle

## 8 Hours

Raymond

Born two months too early
To a mother of nineteen

In those 28 weeks,
You were beginning to dream
to hiccup
to make faces in the womb
showing you were developing
a slapstick sense of humor.

You had a 90% chance of living outside
the comfort of your amniotic sack

And you did live.

Your mother
watched your lungs take
in oxygen and push it out

You looked at her.

You stuck out your tongue.
You stayed in your mother's arms.

As the minutes passed into hours,
we all thought you would keep going,
keep breathing, keep living.

By hour 8, you gave us all the joy
and love you could. You were
passing from this world into the next

leaving your earthbound family
with a void they will never try to fill again.

---

MM Wittle is a literacy coach by day, an adjunct professor at night, and a writer on Sundays. Visit the musing of MM Wittle at https://www.mmwittle.com and check out her creative nonfiction memoir Three Decades and I'm Gone published by Creeping Lotus Press.

# Paul-Victor Winters

## Peter Onion
*For Peter E. Murphy*

There is a man. Inside the man is an orb, little and yellowed. It's sandwiched between his gallbladder and tired gut. Inside the orb, of course, is a village. A townful of people and stories.
A dusty town with more coffee shops than needed. Monday trash pickup. A town council only somewhat corrupt. In one shop, an old couple smelling of orange peels stock hand-knitted socks onto shelves. In another, a woman with white eyes—really, white eyes—plays vintage vinyl on vintage turntables. It's a hip town.
They skip Tuesdays. No such thing as a Tuesday. Everyone in the town speaks Welsh, but only to their paramours, and everyone's surname is Onion. They celebrate secular holidays as though they were religious holidays and religious holidays as though they were secular. They share and speak kindly to one another, mostly.
"G'morning, Mr. Onion." "Hey, there, Onion." "Welcome to Onion's Bar & Grill." "Happy Onion Day!"

The man himself suffers heartburn and melancholy. The man himself suspects the village, this snow-globe of his, but he refuses the MRIs; he tries not to think of it and tries not to complain. Why so many stories? He isn't sure. You? You will see him at the Post Office or bakery. You must say nothing of the town. Do not call him Mr. Mayor. He's busy listening to the lilting chatter, the hum of all the Onion folk, fussing about busily, the poor wretches.

---

Paul-Victor Winters is a poet from Northwestern Jerscy, transplanted to Southern Jersey. He teaches at Egg Harbor Township High School. His poems can be found in numerous journals.

# Scott Woodland

## First

In that pristinely innocent and distant time,
When a blush was acquiescence
And a hand hold eternity,
In concert with our souls,
And with the Great Soul Herself,
Like Molly Bloom we cried, "YES!"
And flung were we
By our own hands, our own spirits
Onto each other,
With each other,
Through each other ...
Until we were One.
And forever we remain.
And not Time,
Not Man,
Not Calm,
Not Storm,
Not the ever-segregating moments of lonely being -
Nothing -
Nothing –
Nothing –

Can or will -
Tear Us apart.

---

Scott Woodland has been communicating what he sees, mentally cobbles together, and feels since early childhood. He attended Middlebury College and has lived and worked in the cities of New York, Los Angeles, Vienna and Prague.

## About the Editor

James P. Wagner (Ishwa) is an editor, publisher, award-winning fiction writer, essayist, performance poet, and alum twice over (BA & MALS) of Dowling College. He is the publisher for Local Gems Poetry Press and the Senior Founder and President of the Bards Initiative, a Long Island, NY based non-profit dedicated to using poetry for social improvement. He has been on the advisory boards for the Nassau County Poet Laureate Society and the Walt Whitman Birthplace Association. James also helped with the Dowling College Writing Conference.. James believes poetry is alive and well and thoroughly enjoys being a part of poetic culture. His most recent collection of poetry is *Ten Year Reunion*. He is the Long Island, NY National Beat Poet Laureate from 2017-2019. He was the Walt Whitman Bicentennial Convention Chairman. James has edited over 50 poetry anthologies.

Local Gems Poetry Press is a small Long Island based poetry press dedicated to spreading poetry through performance and the written word. Local Gems believes that poetry is the voice of the people, and as the sister organization of the Bards Initiative, believes that poetry can be used to make a difference.

Local Gems has published over 200 titles.

www.localgemspoetrypress.com

Made in the
USA
Lexington, KY